THE SECRET ISLAND

HIDDEN CONTINENTS AND EXTRA TERRITORIES ON OUR TRUE EARTH

Published by Dave James

www.DaveJames.uk

TABLE OF CONTENTS

CHARACTERS

Leon 36
Callum 58
Nadi 34 - Callum's girlfriend
Marau 18 - Nadi's brother
Kona 18 - Marau's best friend
Jita 38 - Rescued Filipina
Lorenzo 95 - Taxi driver on Galeca
Gallen 178 - Elder on Galeca
Kiers Harrison - Governor of Galeca
Gavay 168 - Owner of the shop on Faerfeng Bay

Yachts
Mermaid - Callum's 110 feet motor sailing yacht
Sayang - Leon's charter 52 feet sailing yacht

PROLOGUE

Since 1971 over 90 U.S. banks with over a billion dollars in assets have failed. The banking crash was planned long ago and when Leon heard that the Silicon Valley Bank had collapsed, he knew it was time to get out before the dominoes started to fall.

With several million in stocks, bonds and shares, he sold them all and bought physical gold, silver and crypto currencies, with most going into the privacy coins such as Monero, Dero and Pirate Chain. Still a fairly young man at 36, Leon had never married due to his high pressure lifestyle as a currency trader with the London Merchant Bank.

However, his passion for travel, yachts and exploration brought him in contact with Callum, another British adventurer from Weymouth in England. They met in a small bar on the island of Namaku while both independently cruising the Fiji archipelago. Callum 58 was already retired and living with his long term girlfriend Nadi 34, also from Fiji on "Mermaid", his stunning 110 feet custom motor sailing yacht with 5 staterooms and accommodation for 10 guests with 7 crew. Callum also had a high net worth from selling a software company he founded 20 years earlier and found Leon to be a very interesting character.

CHAPTER 1

CALLUM AND LEON

The conversation was often about yachts and Callum wanted to know why Leon was sailing alone, albeit with 2 crew in the South Pacific on Sayang, a beautiful 52ft sailing yacht. Leon explained that he was only chartering Sayang until he decided where to live and what to purchase. Nadi then asked why he was cruising around Fiji as it was so remote?

"I just love islands I suppose, I've cruised the Maldives and Seychelles and wanted to check out Fiji, Tonga, the Cook islands and then French Polynesia. I'm also looking for a safe haven, somewhere to build a nice cabin overlooking the ocean and to be my main cruising base," Leon replied.

"There are some beautiful plots available in Tonga, we looked at some in Vavu Vavu and you can get an acre on the hillside with stunning views for a couple of thousand dollars with a monthly lease payment of $65 on a rolling 33 year lease up to 99 years," Callum said, rubbing his chin as he still wondered why did didn't buy a plot when he had the chance.

"Sounds great, but I'm not ready to settle down just yet, too much exploring to do but I'll know it when I find it."

"Did you know that Japan recently announced that they found

7000 new islands? That means the number of their islands has doubled with over 14,000 now included on its map! How the hell can 7000 islands have been hidden for so long and why reveal it now!"

"Really, so when did you hear about that?" Leon asked.

"I think they announced it in January 2023 and what about the Pacific and Southern Oceans, there are certain areas that nobody sails in, such as the lower latitudes between New Zealand and Santiago, Chile. You have Bora Bora and the islands you mentioned but if you switch the layers to satellite on Google maps, there are many islands that are Photoshopped and blurred out in the lower latitudes between New Zealand and Chile!" Callum replied.

"So have you looked around that area then?"

"Yes but the further South one goes, all the conventional maps are wrong, distances and compass bearings are not accurate. The Southern Ocean is far bigger than they want us to know about and some of the older maps show huge continents in those regions. Maybe they were submerged during the last great reset like Atlantis and Lemuria."

"Reset!"

"Yes every 140 years approximately, there are resets like world wide floods or mud floods like in the early 1900's. You must have seen the many buildings in the UK but also the USA and many other countries with windows below the ground level?"

"Yes... I've always wondered why they built them like that, so you're saying there was some kind of mud flood that buried them?"

"Yes, there are thousands of videos online, just type in mud floods or check out, "My Lunch Break" on YouTube or "John Levi" who also has a great channel, if they are still there as the powers that be are censoring and hiding our real history. But getting back to hidden islands, have you ever heard of Kiribati?" Callum asked.

"Never heard of it, why?"

"Kiribati is a tiny country or more like a sandbar in the middle of nowhere and huge container ships are registered there that have been seen on the maritime route finders websites to be hundreds of miles within Antarctica!"

"What do you mean, within Antarctica? It's all solid ice isn't it?"

"Exactly, that's what they want us to believe, we are told that Antarctica is all ice, so how are huge container ships being seen on the tracking websites, hundreds of miles within Antarctica!"

"Now that is interesting but I thought there was an Antarctic treaty that states, No one can independently explore or go below 60 % latitude!"

"Correct, but some people claim there are hidden shipping lanes to continents beyond Antarctica. Have you seen the old Shingon Buddhist map brought from China to Japan in the 9th century? It's basically showing many more continents beyond Antarctica, which means that, either the earth is a thousand times bigger than we've been led to believe or the true earth is a non rotating extended plane."

Was This World Map Made Ten Centuries Ago?

POLITICIANS AND JOB CHASERS DISAPPOINTED

SOME DETAILS OF GREAT STORM

FRED CHURCH'S FATHER SCOURGES OLD MASTERS

Shingon Buddhist map showing many more continents beyond Antarctica the two outer rings

"So looking at that Buddhist map it makes perfect sense, Antarctica is not all ice like Google Earth depicts and when you zoom in, it's all Photoshopped to hide our true reality. I seriously believe there are shipping lanes to the outer lands," Callum declared.

"What! So you believe there are more continents beyond Antarctica?"

"Yes, but we only know about the continents in the middle of our world pond out to Australia. They created the Antarctic treaty which forbids anyone exploring beyond the 60 degree parallel and to stop independent travel. There are British naval bases on all the islands and other countries around the supposed Antarctic ice wall that stop anyone trying to go into the banned regions, so what are they hiding?

"Extra Territory or more land!" Leon replied.

"Exactly! The Pacific covers 165 million square kilometres, which is larger than the landmass of every single continent and island we know of combined. And why do many World leaders, Popes and individuals high up in the control game like John Kerry keep visiting Antarctica, disappear for a couple of days, then return! There's definitely something going on down there and maybe that's where the true controllers of our world actually live and some claim they are not even human."

"I can believe that with everything happening in the world over the last few years, It wouldn't surprise me at all if they lived outside our open prison."

"Yes and even if we had the resources and could go out to explore beyond the 60 degree parallel, we'd need a huge ship and they don't even allow us to carry extra fuel, so exploring beyond Antarctica is definitely off limits."

"So what's your plan then?" Leon asked inquisitively.

"I have no doubt in my mind that there is more land beyond Antarctica, however, I think they are hiding islands or even a whole continent in the South Pacific, think about it, if you look at the Gleason's map, there is a huge area that virtually nobody crosses. Did you know that southern ocean sea captains always report that the distances and compass bearings are always wrong the further south one goes! Of which, makes a lot more sense on these maps."

"So what you're saying is, we're in a people farm or a giant prison with Antarctica as our no go boundary?"

"No, the boundary is 60 degrees South which is still about a thousand miles from Antarctica and what the hell are those giant container ships transporting to or from the outer lands? Could it be technology, resources, food, maybe even children!"

"What! you mean like child trafficking?"

"I have no idea but not only children, millions of people go missing every year, and what about all the orphan trains that brought thousands of children to the World Fairs after the last great reset? So, God knows what's really going on! I mean, whoever heard of Kiribati and why did the Chinese government give them 10 Billion dollars last year? It's just a tiny sand bar in the middle of nowhere, obviously something is going on!"

"Wow... you two can talk and you've only had a couple of beers, are we going to order the seafood buffet you promised me?" Nadi asked Callum.

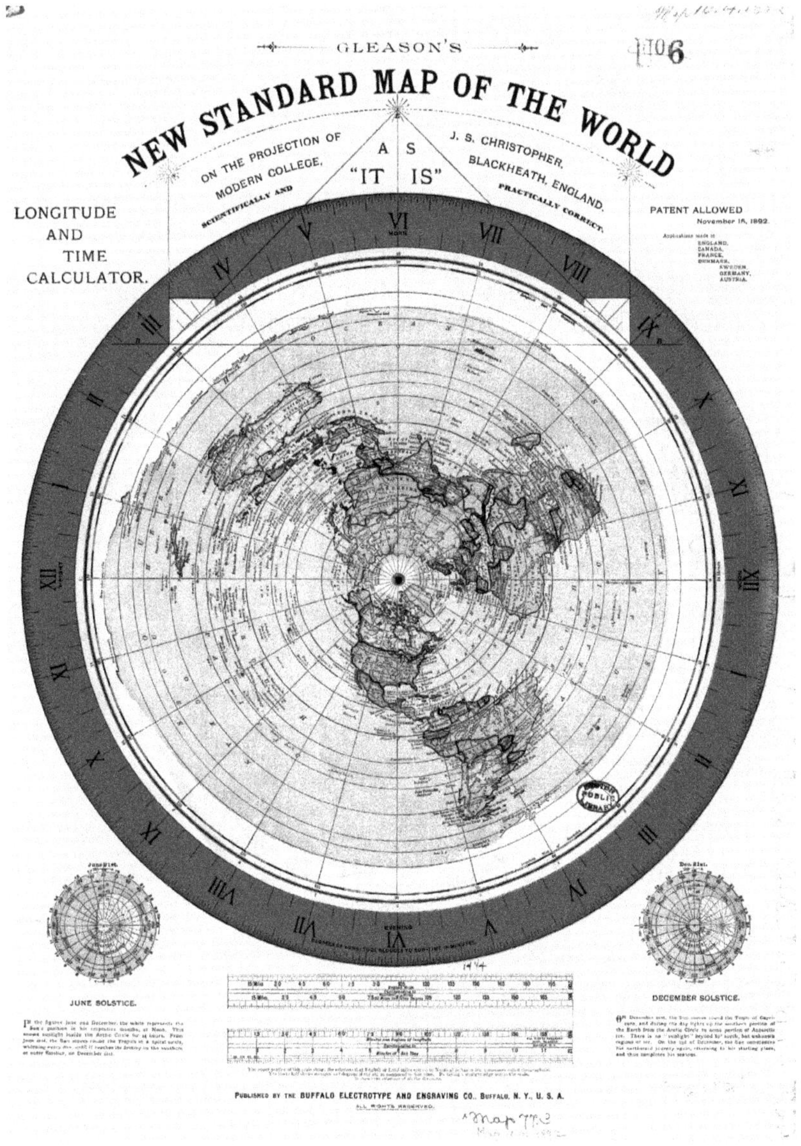
GLEASON'S
NEW STANDARD MAP OF THE WORLD
ON THE PROJECTION OF MODERN COLLEGE, SCIENTIFICALLY AND
A S
"IT IS"
J. S. CHRISTOPHER, BLACKHEATH, ENGLAND, PRACTICALLY CORRECT.
LONGITUDE AND TIME CALCULATOR.
PATENT ALLOWED
November 16, 1892.
Applications made in
ENGLAND,
CANADA,
FRANCE,
DENMARK,
SWEDEN,
GERMANY,
AUSTRIA.
JUNE SOLSTICE.
DECEMBER SOLSTICE.
PUBLISHED BY THE BUFFALO ELECTROTYPE AND ENGRAVING CO., BUFFALO, N. Y., U. S. A.
ALL RIGHTS RESERVED.

CHAPTER 2

THE PLAN

Leon had never met anyone like Callum before and reminded him of Harrison Ford's character in his adventure movie, Raiders of the Lost Arc. Callum also looked the part and Leon was pleased to have met and made friends with him.

"So how long have you chartered your yacht for?" Callum asked Leon.

"It's on a rolling monthly basis and I've been cruising around these waters for six weeks now."

"And where are you going next?"

"I thought I'd venture out to Niue then Palmerston and the Cook Islands," Leon replied.

"Well, I've done all those several times now and the Cook Islands are on the tropic of Capricorn at 20 degrees South. But I wanted to ask what you thought about our conversation yesterday evening, I haven't met many people like yourself that were interested or open minded enough to discuss this topic with."

"Same here, most people I know are trapped in the matrix and totally mind controlled by the main stream media, but yes, I found your knowledge on the subject fascinating."

"How would you like to join Nadi and I on a new expedition? It's not worth taking two yachts so you could have a cabin on ours and save yourself a heap of chartering fees." Callum offered.

"So where are you planning to explore?"

"Like I said last night, there's a vast expanse of ocean below the Cook islands at 20 degrees latitude and even at 40 - 50 degrees, there could still be hidden islands as New Zealand and the Southern part of Argentina still has liveable weather where plants and wildlife can flourish and survive. But beyond 60 degrees, it becomes too cold and lifeless, so pointless us exploring there unless we take a chance and head South and try to find an opening in the supposed, Antarctic ice wall."

"So, you don't subscribe to Antarctica being a continent at the bottom of the globe then?" Leon asked.

"Definitely not, like I said yesterday, if anything, the earth that we know is an extended plane or it has to be thousands of times bigger than they are telling us. Look, I have some very interesting maps if you want to discuss the lands beyond Antarctica but I still believe they are hiding islands or even a huge continent in the southern ocean between 60 and 40 degrees latitude."

"OK, so if I decide to come with you, does Nadi have a sister or any attractive friends that like yachts and expeditions?" Leon joked.

"All her sisters are married, yet there are lots of available women on the islands but whether they want to spend months on a yacht is the biggest issue, but I see where you're coming from and I suppose I'm really lucky to have found Nadi."

"I can ask around," Nadi said smiling.

"Hey, I was only joking and the last thing I want is to break some poor girls heart. I'm not ready to settle down yet, however, a similar minded female companion would be nice, provided we are compatible and my personal preference is, I only like skinny to normal but most of the island girls are a little too plump for my liking!" Leon said as Callum and Nadi smiled at each other.

"All joking aside, yes I'd love to join you on Mermaid for an expedition with or without a girlfriend. My monthly lease agreement is up for renewal in two weeks time but I can always end it early if you want to set sail sooner."

"Let's give it another week or so here in Fiji and we can get all the supplies we need for a long trip stowed on board. You can choose one of the other four staterooms and move aboard whenever you like. Best to see how we all get on before a long trip, nothing worse than being on a yacht in the middle of nowhere with someone you don't get on with, especially a woman!" he said smiling.

"That's why I travel alone, so maybe it's not a good idea looking for a girlfriend,"Leon replied.

"My thoughts exactly, leave it in the hands of the gods, the right one will appear exactly when she is supposed to."

"Wise words, so how long have you and Nadi been together?"

"It must be getting on for five years now and she's like a dream come true, we never argue and seem to have the same thoughts and opinions about most things. And to be perfectly honest, I wasn't looking for anyone and she just seemed to appear one day while I was stocking up for another trip. Long story and maybe I'll tell you all about it over a beer or two."

CHAPTER 3

THE MAPS

As they sat down and Callum pulled out all his maps, Leon asked,

"So what in your opinion is the best map to use for sailing the southern oceans then?"

"Well, I've studied many maps and the most accurate for distances and navigation is the Gleason's - New Standard Map of the World or the 1945 Air map which is very similar. However, did you know that the Gleason's map was in every school and text book prior to Admiral Byrd discovering the land beyond the poles? And after mentioning his discoveries on TV on The Chronoscope Chronicles, he met an untimely death of a suspected heart attack and the Antarctic treaty was quickly put in place. The Rockefeller's then introduced the globe model in all schools and the Gleason's maps were removed and even text book references to it have disappeared."

"Sounds like the controllers want to keep everyone in the dark!" Leon replied.

"Of course and then there is the 1587 Urbano Monte map of the world showing the four large islands at the North Pole and many other lands surrounding our continents, of which, have now all been Photoshopped out by the powers that should not be and Google of course. Try zooming in on the North Pole or Antarctica and all you get is CGI and cartoons, they show a few areas around the edge but its totally different to the old maps."

"So what do you think they are hiding?" Leon asked.

"Extra territory of course, so, if there were people who lived in the extra territory, what would we call them?"

"No idea!"

"Extraterrestrials who come from the outer space."

"My God! That's so much more believable than extraterrestrials coming from planets light years away only to crash in Roswell!"

"Exactly, all made up tales to keep the prison planet globe lie going. I believe we are in some kind of people farm but a small group individuals at the top know exactly what's going on. So back to your question about the maps, for what we are planning to do the Gleason's map is probably the most accurate. However, as we are on the subject of maps, have you ever come across Vibes of Cosmos and the Moon Map of the Earth?

"Never heard of it."

"Well, he has lots of videos on YouTube and it's uncannily accurate. He zooms in and shows the different areas of the Moon map that correspond almost perfectly with the Gleason's map, but it also shows large continents in the Pacific and outside the Antarctic ice wall areas. One in particular was Lemuria which is between Australia and South America and is huge but not showing on our current maps or the Gleason's map. So in my opinion, it could be a submerged continent and all the small Pacific Islands we have now like Fiji, Tonga, Cook islands etc. are remnants of a far bigger continent now submerged under the water. And because of it's position and size, it would be far too difficult to hide as anyone sailing across the Pacific would come across it for sure. But, when one looks at the lower latitudes below the tropic of Capricorn, there are several smaller land masses, each about the size of New Zealand. Now, on our Gleason's map, the lowest islands shown are Rapu or Easter Island, Pitcairn and a few others but below that it's just thousands of miles of empty ocean. So, if they were going to hide extra land, where we still get warm enough temperatures, that is where I want to search."

"Can you show me these maps?" Leon asked.

Callum pulled out his high resolution copy of the Gleason's map and one of the Moon maps to show him the extra land and then said,

"And there is a strange clock in London that shows the exact same map but with an inner circle of the path of Sun that migrates outwards or around the greater map of continents every twenty odd thousand years or so."

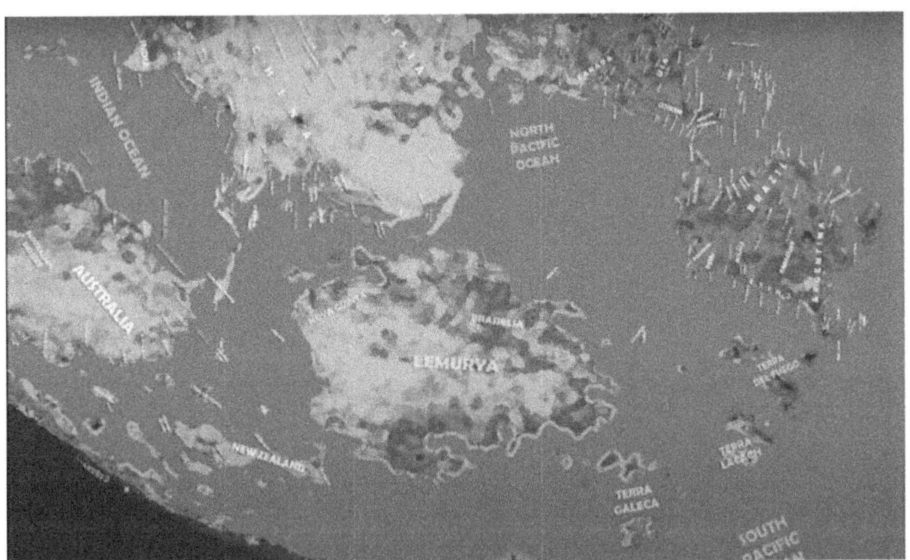

Moon map showing Lemuria between Australia, New Zealand and South America

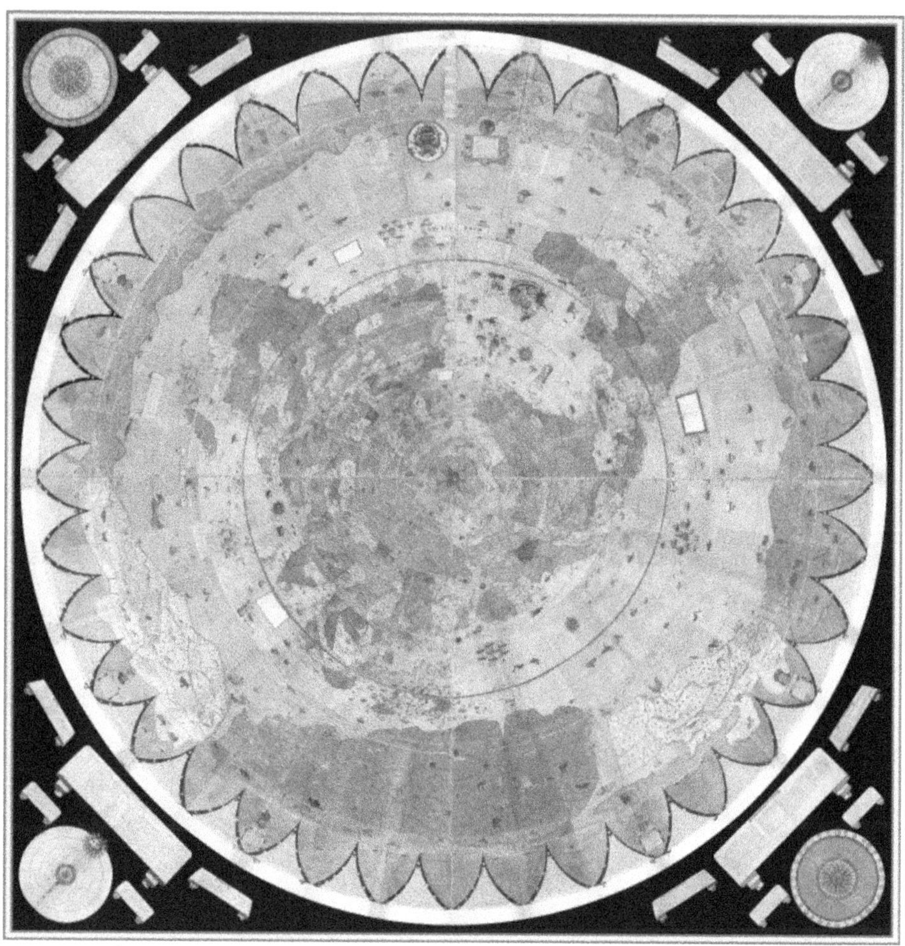

1587 Urbano Monte map of the world

"This makes perfect sense if the world was bigger than they tell us but didn't Captain Cook try to sail around Antarctica?" Leon asked.

"Yes and if it was a continent at the bottom of a ball at 13,000 miles total circumference, why did it take Captain Cook three and a half years and cover over 60,000 miles! But it works perfectly on the Gleason's map because Antarctica is not a continent at the bottom of a ball covered in ice and spinning at a 1000 miles per hour at the equator, it is the shoreline that holds all our oceans in, like a giant lake and all the continents are like giant islands within the lake. And before you say the pre programmed response word "Gravity", that we all believed was true before opening our minds and using actual critical thinking and looking at reality in nature. No way can trillions of tons of water and giant ships be stuck to the side of a spinning water ball when a butterfly can just take off and fly around and even the wind flows in different directions. Their magical gravity has never been proven and is all so ludicrous once you look into it. In fact, without gravity, the entire globe model falls apart."

"But on this Moon map, I've never heard of Terra Galeca, Lacach or Del Fuego!"

"Exactly, and look at their latitude, they would have the same climate as New Zealand but much lower than any shipping or sailing route."

"So, if I was to sail from Chile to New Zealand, I'd plot a course to hit Pitcairn or Tahiti and all the other islands at higher latitudes." Leon said.

"Of course, why would anyone plot a course down there where there are thousands of miles of nothing but ocean and no land or islands on any maps! Only a mad man would plot a course missing all the known islands."

"So you're the madman then," Leon joked as Callum put the maps away and pulled out another map.

"Now this one is interesting because it shows all the British Crown military bases protecting the 60 degree Antarctic treaty. Australia, New Zealand, South Africa are quite obvious but they also have bases in Pitcairn, South Georgia, St Helens, British Indian Ocean Territory and now we know why the Falklands was such a strategic group of islands and they went to war with Argentina."

"So what happens if someone like us strays down to the 60 degree zone?"

"Apparently they have warning buoys, aircraft, drones and warships intercepting anyone who dares to go down there, but interestingly for us, there doesn't seem to be anything between Pitcairn and New Zealand, which is, in my estimation looking at the Gleason's map, some 5000+ miles but Google and various online calculators claim it is only 3464 miles. Either way, that's a huge expanse of nothingness to protect, unless of course there is something in between."

"I can see why you want to check it out but what if they have warships and aircraft based there as well?"

"I don't know but my guess is, there is a secret continent or a group of islands where many of the high profile celebrities and people like Epstein that faked their deaths are living now and laughing at us."

Leon was struggling to keep up with all the information Callum was revealing but deep down inside, his intuition had never let him down and felt that Callum was right over the target. Nadi had gone ashore to visit her family leaving Callum and Leon to chat and have a few beers.

CHAPTER 4

WORLD NEWS

When Nadi returned from shore, she handed Callum a newspaper.

"What's this?" He asked curiously.

"Look at the headline, the psychopath controllers are in a panic!"

Callum read the article then handed it to to Leon.

Rouge military SWAT teams from UK and Europe eliminate top WEF and WHO leaders.

WEF (World Economic Forum) leaders are in a panic after a rogue SWAT team staged a surprise attack in Davos, Switzerland. Eight high profile leaders and advisors were killed in a military style coordinated attack. Video footage has been released showing the victims executed with a bullet in their head in front of their followers. A strong message was also broadcast saying that all WEF and WHO (World Health Organisation) members in positions of government or control will be the next targets unless they step down immediately and relinquish all association with the WEF and WHO. The SWAT teams are rumoured to be working under a deposed president, that for obvious reasons needs to remain anonymous.

"About time someone with balls targeted these unelected control freaks trying to enslave the world," Callum said to Leon.

"Yeah but they already control so many countries and even that WEF Schwab guy said on video, they have already infiltrated most governments and control many of the cabinet with his young global leaders. And to be honest, I was expecting something like this to happen a long time ago and one of the reasons I got out of banking and trading, the word amongst all traders is that they are going to crash the dollar which will affect all other currencies and plunge the world into chaos," Leon replied.

"So you decided to get out of the mass mind controlled UK while you could and find a nice little island safe haven?"

"Yeah or get a nice yacht like yours to live on and cruise around the lesser populated areas of the world and I suppose a lot of the psycho elites will be running to hide in their bunkers now."

"Or run to their luxury safe havens on the secret lands, which could be a good or bad thing depending on how you look at it. Good if they head out on their private jets or mega yachts because we could maybe watch where they go via radar or long range optics, if we're close enough to their destination. And bad because wherever these secret islands are, they will be on high alert and obviously have their own private armies of mercenaries to protect them."

Nadi was listening patiently and then said that everyone on Fiji were excited at the news and apparently the Fijian president Wiliame Katonivere had gone into hiding as he too was a WEF puppet.

"Interesting, it wouldn't surprise me if it was that Brazilian guy, Bolsanero I think his name was that had the election stolen from him by another WEF puppet they released from jail."

"So talking of radar, what kind of system are you using on Mermaid then?"

"I have a Simrad marine radar system with an approximate range of 50 miles under good atmospheric conditions but out there in the southern ocean it's nowhere near as good as my Nikon P1000 with a special infra red lens conversion and I can see well over 500 miles in an air plane or about 200 miles over the ocean on a super clear day."

"But that's impossible, what about the curvature of the earth? Leon asked curiously.

"What curvature! If you do a search online about distance and curvature, all you get is disinformation but there are thousands of videos online explaining that curvature doesn't exist. If you use the standard globe curvature formula which is 8 inches per mile squared, a 6 foot person standing at the edge of calm water, should not be able to see anything beyond 3 miles as there would be a 6 feet drop our horizon, however, we can see much further than that, take lighthouses as a classic example, we can see a lighthouse over a hundred miles away, so how is that possible if there is curvature! Navy gunners have reported being able to laser pinpoint a target at over 100 miles away, submarine captains also report being able to use sonar for 100 miles plus, both impossible if there were any curvature. But with infra red attached to a good zoom camera, it cuts through the thickness of the atmosphere and shows boats, planes and land hundreds of miles away! So, I can assure you Leon there is zero curvature but I don't want to get into all that as it's basically a subject that triggers people no end. We've all been conditioned or brainwashed via schools and the TV programming to believe in the globe model, but that's all it is, an elaborate cartoon model that has been created to keep the control of the masses in the hands of the few."

"But what about boats disappearing over the horizon?" Leon

asked.

"Really! Next time you think you see that happening, grab a pair of binoculars or a good zoom camera like my P1000, zoom in and it will still be there, it's simply perspective as your eyes cannot see forever, everything in the distance converges into the horizon. Take an aircraft flying overhead, as it goes away, it gets smaller and lower in the sky until it basically disappears. You cannot see any further than where the clouds or sky meet the ground or water unless you zoom in and increase your angular resolution."

"Interesting."

"OK, so let's find out what Nadi is cooking in the galley, smells delicious."

As they sat around the dining table, Leon asked why Callum chose Fiji as his island base?

"Because Fiji consists of about 330 islands, of which, about 110 are permanently inhabited then there are more than 500 islets, amounting to a total land area of about 7,100 square miles. I could live here forever if it wasn't for my burning desire to know the truth about the world and where we actually live. I know without any doubt in my mind, they are hiding more land.

"But who are THEY?" Leon asked.

"Look, obviously a very small group of people, if they really are human, control all the governments, the Convid bullshit and worldwide lockdowns proved that. I think they are even higher up in the pecking order than Klaus Schwab of the WEF, but now he's been taken out, they, whoever they are, will simply place another puppet in his role. They will never reveal themselves, especially now the people are waking up and some of their top spokespersons have been eliminated. I find it interesting because you would think that all the royal families would be in the know, but I have a friend living in Thailand who said that 80% of the country are still believing in the fictional virus scam-demic and wearing masks. One of the princesses also had three shots and last anyone heard she was in a coma. Either the King is not in the know or if he is, failed to tell his immediate family of the worldwide democide plan."

"Yes I heard about that as well."

CHAPTER 5

SETTING SAIL

A week later

Callum was still on the lookout for two more crew members as the Mermaid needed at least five crew to sail her, not including Nadi and keep watch on a rota system. His issue being, not wanting to take anyone on board for such a long voyage without knowing them well. Leon was an exception as they both shared the same vision and Callum saw a younger version of himself in Leon.

Leon had ended his agreement with the charter company and his yacht had disembarked back to base with the crew. Now moved onboard Mermaid, he asked Callum when he intended to set sail?

"I'd leave today if we had enough crew but the two young guys that I've taken out in the past are both married and understandably, don't want to leave their wives and children for such a long and possibly dangerous expedition. But Nadi has a young 18 year old brother and maybe he has a friend that would be interested, she's with him onshore now asking around."

The Mermaid was ready to sail and when Nadi returned with her brother and another young man of similar age, Callum sat down with them for a chat.

"OK we set sail tomorrow morning at sunrise," Callum announced as Nadi hugged him saying thank you.

Marau and Kona were best friends and loved sailing but had zero long term prospects on Fiji. Callum had taken Marau out several times before and knew he was trustworthy, explained all the risks and that they could be at sea for many months and if they did find what they were looking for, may not even return to Fiji. His offer of 2000 Fijian dollars per month (£700) was far more than they could ever have expected and both accepted the offer immediately. Taking the tender back to shore, Marau and Kona went to say goodbye to their families and collect any personal belongings they needed.

At first light, Callum had already been up for several hours and rang the ships bell to wake up the rest of the crew. Everyone appeared on deck as Callum explained the ships rules, the most important one being, he was the captain and had the final decision in any issue or dispute. A rotating 6 hour watch was set up between all 4 crew members excluding Nadi as her role was cooking and cleaning and general ships chores.

The first heading was South East towards Tonga which was about 400 nautical miles and then head South until they were at the same latitude as mid New Zealand and then head East another 2 to 3 days or 1000 miles. Everyone was excited as they set sail and the first few days were uneventful, however, on the forth day, Marau said he thought he saw a boat on the horizon. Callum pulled out his binoculars and saw a sailing boat some 20 odd miles away with a broken mast.

"There you go, this is a classic example of a boat we should not be able to see, as according to globe maths, it should be well below the horizon and the supposed curvature of the earth but using binoculars, there it is, it's simply the resolution limit of our eyes not curvature," Callum said, handing Leon the binoculars.

Sailing towards the stricken vessel, they soon found it also had a huge hole in the side, just above the waterline and looked like it had been shot at. Nobody was on deck so after calling out, Callum decided to pull up alongside. Callum and Leon boarded the yacht and found a man and a woman laying unconscious down below. Rushing up to get some water, Leon came back and found that the woman was coming around but seemed to be delirious and talking nonsense. Handing Callum a bottle of water, he helped the woman take a few sips, then grabbing the bottle, she drank it all and tried to wake up her partner.

Callum then told her that the man was dead and there was nothing they could do. Bursting into tears, she said they'd been attacked by a military drone and that she and her husband had been drifting for about 5 weeks. They were able to survive by catching fish but when the drinking water ran out, things became so desperate, they started drinking their own urine. Helping her onboard the Mermaid, Callum explained that they couldn't take her dead husband as they were on an expedition but would report the yachts location as soon as they were within radio range but that was not going to be anytime soon. She wasn't understanding what was happening and suddenly jumped overboard as they started sailing away from the stricken yacht.

Leon dived in after her and they managed to get her back onboard with Nadi's help and quickly took her down to the galley where Nadi gave her some, bananas, soup and bread. After a good feed she told them her name was Jita and that the man on the yacht was her German husband Gert. She spoke fairly good English and said that she was from Boracay in the Philippines and had met her husband in Germany. Asking what they were doing out there? She said her husband used to work for the German government and was obsessed with Antarctica and Lemuria.

"But Lemuria is supposedly a sunken continent!" Callum exclaimed.

"Not true, Gert said there was a group of secret islands that are not shown on any world map and the German government has a military base there," Jita replied.

"But what happened to your yacht?" Leon asked.

"We were attacked by a drone, it just appeared and fired on us, we hid down below but when we came up, the mast was broken and we couldn't call for help because we were in the restricted area."

"What do you mean restricted area?"

"I don't know but Gert said we were almost at the destination and then the drone appeared and was shooting at us."

"So what map were you using?" Callum asked.

"The Moon map, Gert said it was the only true map of the earth."

Deciding that they needed to see exactly what map they were using, Callum turned around and sailed back to their stricken yacht. After retrieving the map, they realised that it was all in German and the German government were obviously well aware of the extra land not showing on all other maps. But more interestingly, was the large amount of land and continents that were outside of the supposed Antarctica ice wall. Asking Jita what else Gert had told her she said,

"The Moon map had been verified by the German government as extremely accurate and that our Sun only circled the tropics of Cancer and Capricorn but over thousands of years, our magnetic North Pole was also moving in a smaller circle which meant that, in the next few hundred years, the earth that we know now will be experiencing an ice age and the land currently not known about beyond Antarctica by the majority of our world, would be experiencing weather like our world now."

"So, you mean the Sun migrates outwards?" Leon asked.

"No, Gert said that the Sun rotates around us like you said but the magnetic North Pole also moves in great circle around the whole of the flat earth every 26,000 years."

"So he believed it to be flat and not a globe?" Leon asked as Callum stood there smiling.

"Of course, it is scientifically impossible to have a 1000 miles per hour rotating water planet in a void or vacuum and he said that gravity is the second biggest lie. The German government have much knowledge on this and have been in Antarctica since the 1940's. They have submarine bases and Gert said there are millions of people living in the outer lands beyond Antarctica."

"Oh My God, that's incredible!" Nadi exclaimed.

"Yes but he also said there is so much deception in the world, Gert was very high up in government and as soon as he retired, he wanted to go find the remaining islands of Lemuria."

"But why was he so obsessed?" Callum asked.

"Because they have free energy, people do not get sick and Gert had cancer," Jita replied and started sobbing again.

CHAPTER 6

CONVERSATION WITH JITA

Over the next few days, Callum tried to get more information out of Jita but she kept on saying that Gert was the one with all the knowledge and not her. Callum was even more convinced that more land existed after hearing Jita's account and had been spending hours talking with her about her life with Gert and why she also believed in his obsession.

"So tell me Jita, how did you meet Gert?" Callum asked.

"I was 27 and working at the hospital in Stuttgart and Gert was coming in for tests, then one day he invited me to dinner and we married 6 months later."

"So how old are you now? If you don't mind me asking."

"I'm 38 why?"

"Because you don't look 38, I'd have guessed you were 28, so how old was Gert then?"

"He was 58."

"So you were 20 years younger than him?"

"Yes."

"And do you have a house or anything back in Germany?"

"No, he sold everything when he retired and bought the boat?"

"I see, so you were into sailing with him then?"

"No, I hate boats but he was my husband and if I did not go with him, I would be all alone in Germany, so would have probably have had to go back to the Philippines."

Leon was intrigued with her story and later, while pondering over the new German Moon map, Callum said,

"But what I cannot understand is, why they were attacked by a drone, they were nowhere near the 60 degree parallel which is much lower than New Zealand at 45 degrees, unless it was launched from an island they almost found. According to their map, there is a large island about the size of Hawaii's big island which is about 50 miles wide, 1200 miles South of where we found them but they had been drifting for weeks and why didn't the drone finish the job and sink them!"

"So where's Kiribati on their map?" Leon asked.

"Right there," Callum pointed as they both looked at each other and smiled.

"But why does the International Date Line make that weird shape over Kiribati?"

"Because when they created the globe, by wrapping a flat earth map around a ball, they had to compress all the Southern Oceans, which also made Antarctica a small island at the bottom, hence all the distances are always wrong and if we really did live on a spinning globe, all the time zones should be straight lines, this is yet another proof that when the Rockefeller's took out of all the text books the Gleason's map and introduced the fictitious globe map, of which, there are so many variations, they had to create the strange looking International Date Line."

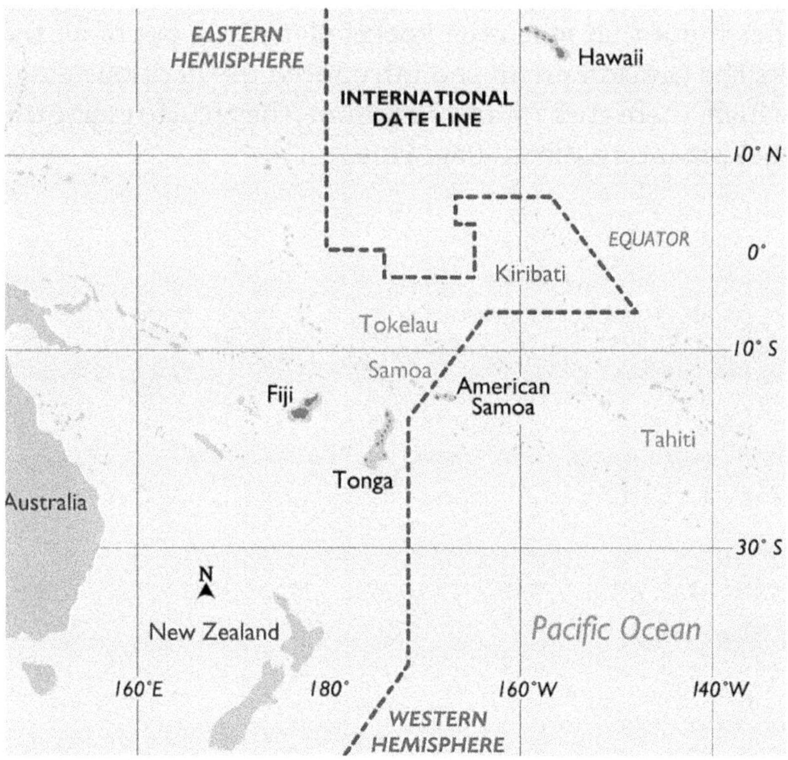
EASTERN
HEMISPHERE
INTERNATIONAL
DATE LINE
Hawaii
10° N
EQUATOR
0°
Kiribati
Tokelau
10° S
Samoa
American
Samoa
Fiji
Tahiti
Tonga
Australia
30° S
N
New Zealand
Pacific Ocean
160°E
180°
160°W
140°W
WESTERN
HEMISPHERE

Kiribati was almost directly in line with the new group of islands on the German Moon map, so Callum called everyone together and explained what they had found. Everyone except Jita was in agreement that they needed to proceed to 160 degrees West Longitude, then head South to the new island Terra Galeca on the German Moon map at 50 degrees latitude, below and the East of New Zealand. Callum also told Jita that she could disembark to another boat or land if they came across any but the expedition must continue.

CHAPTER 7

TERRA GALECA

The next few days were uneventful until a cargo ship was spotted by Kona in the distance. Picking up his binoculars, Callum then said,

"Well it's definitely heading South and around 160 degrees West but it's a huge container ship and there's another ship about half its size following a few miles behind."

Handing the binoculars to Leon, he then said,

"I suggest we keep our distance and steer a course to come in line behind the smaller ship."

Everyone was excited as Callum changed course to follow them. Three hours later they were behind the smaller boat but after zooming in with his super zoom Sony P1000 camera, Callum turned to Leon and said,

"That's Lana, Bill Gates yacht, what the hell! That evil son of a bitch has been in hiding since releasing all the genetically modified mosquitoes and bringing Malaria back to the United States!"

"So you think he's onboard then?" Leon replied.

"Most likely, but I'm more interested in that massive container ship he's following, I wonder what they are transporting and to where!"

"Keeping a good 60 miles behind, to stay off the other ships radar, Jita was becoming more and more anxious as Nadi tried her best to calm her down but she was scared of being attacked again. As nightfall descended and the big red Sun disappeared into the atmospheric deck of opacity on the horizon, Leon was on watch and spotted the Lana heading South East as the container ship continued South. Quickly calling Callum who was down below with Nadi and the rest of the crew, Callum rushed up to the bridge and grabbing the binoculars he took a long observation and then said,

"We are only about 600 miles from the secret island which is obviously where the Lana is heading but where the hell is that container ship going!"

Leon took the binoculars back and continued scanning the two boats, slowly separating in the distance.

Then about fifteen minutes later,

"Oh shit, there's another ship heading towards us," Leon said handing the binoculars to Callum.

Grabbing the binoculars, Callum had a look then said,

"I think it's a warship, better tell the crew."

The British Frigate HMS Sutherland was a type 23, Duke Class, anti submarine warfare vessel but had a wide range of uses. As it approached, everyone assembled on deck and hoped they were not going to be attacked. Callum then received a radio message on the

VHF emergency channel 16.

What is the name of your vessel and how many people onboard?

We are the Mermaid and have 6 people onboard, one is a survivor we picked up that needs medical attention, Callum replied.

What is your destination?

We are heading to Terra Galeca.

You have permission to proceed, however, the marina and dock is full, follow Lana, the ship on your bow and drop anchor in the bay away from the marina entrance.

Callum turned to everyone with a huge smile on his face,

"I have no idea what the hell is going on but that was too easy."

"Look... there's another two ships behind us," Marau said staring through the binoculars.

Callum had another look then said,

"They said the marina was full, so they must think we are residents like Bill Gates and it looks like the authoritarian rats are running from all the violence and upheaval. I can't make out what kind of ships they are but they're obviously heading to the same destination as that evil son of a bitch Gates."

"Good job you remembered Terra Galeca or else we could have been in deep trouble," Leon said, handing the binoculars to Marau.

The Frigate continued on to the ships behind as the Mermaid followed the Lana for another few hours until land was visible on the horizon.

"There it is!" Leon exclaimed, pointing ahead as Callum grabbed the binoculars again.

It was still a good 40 miles to go and everyone was excited, yet apprehensive as they had no idea what to expect on arrival. As they watched, the Lana turned South West towards several other large ships anchored around the entrance to the marina.

"Whatever has happened back home must be very serious for so many mega yachts to be down here, the marina looks like a bloody boat show and the Mermaid must be one of the smallest yachts around. I suggest we all stay onboard and try to suss out how the entry or passport control system works," Callum said seriously.

Dropping the sails and steering the Mermaid under power towards an open area to the East of the marina entrance, they then dropped anchors and watched the two ships behind getting closer.

"Wow, they are almost as big as the Lana," Leon said handing the binoculars to Callum.

Looking at all the super yachts anchored around them, Leon counted 9 not including the Mermaid, then pointing towards another mega yacht, Callum said,

"I think that one is Jeff Bezos yacht Koru and that one behind it is Larry Ellison's yacht Musashi."

"Isn't he the founder of Oracle the US software company?" Leon asked.

"Yes and has a net worth of over 100 Billion and is supposedly the 5th richest person in the world, there must be loads of Billionaires down here!"

"But isn't it strange that none of the crew have become whistleblowers as all these huge yachts must have been here before!" Leon exclaimed.

"Maybe but how would any of them know where they are except the captain and first officer on the bridge, of whom, are probably sworn to secrecy and simply tell the crew they are somewhere else. This could be Tonga or even New Zealand except for those high mountain peaks, it actually does remind me of Hawaii but not as hot."

CHAPTER 8

LORENZO THE DRIVER

After a few hours of watching 3 more ships arriving, including the co-founder of Google, Larry Page's yacht Senses, Callum and Leon were itching to go ashore and explore. So, Callum told Nadi and the rest of the crew to stay on board. Jita was becoming more and more anxious and going on and on about sending a search party out to find her husband Gert. Nadi tried to calm her down by saying they would but first they had to wait until Callum returned.

Taking the tender, Callum and Leon headed ashore, only to find the marina buzzing and packed with mostly 150 meter plus mega yachts. People were wandering around and there was no sign of any police or harbour authorities. Another British warship HMS Defender was also moored up alongside several auxiliary vessels and a submarine tower was also just visible. There was hardly any room to moor up the tender but eventually they managed to double moor next to another small boat and stepped ashore. Walking towards the mainland, they could have been in Puerto Banus or any other wealthy marina, except most of the yachts were huge compared to the Mermaid.

Then they saw two military policemen wandering up and down the main dock carrying machine guns. Waiting until they had passed, Callum and Leon, walked out of the marina and saw a line of white Mercedes with taxi signs on the roof. So, walking over,

Callum asked a driver how much to have a tour of the island?

"No charge for the ride but tips are appreciated, I take it this is your first time to Galeca?"

"Err... Yes, so how big is the island?"

"52 miles from end to end and if you want to take the coast road, you're looking at a good 4 to 5 hours."

The driver seemed friendly enough, so after jumping in the back and hitting the road, Callum asked,

"So how come the taxi ride is free then?"

"Because on Galeca we do not use money, everything can be used or taken from the many stores and supermarkets, we get a monthly credit but we locals also deal between ourselves in US dollars and various other currencies."

"Well driver, I'm Callum and this is Leon, what's your name driver?"

"My name is Lorenzo, nice to meet you." he replied.

"So, what do you mean you deal in currencies but everything is free?"

"Those of us that live here permanently use dollars, mainly for gambling and trading between ourselves."

"So how did you end up living here then?" Leon asked.

"I was born here, like most of the worker class but some have been brought here from the inner lands to service the residents."

"So, do you know anything about the inner lands?"

"You mean like America and Europe, of course, but nobody wants to go live there!"

"Why not?" Leon asked.

"Because of the depopulation program! Everyone on Galeca knows about the mass immigration problems, fluoride in the water and the spraying of the skies to keep all the people dumbed down and easy to control."

"So, how do you know what's going on in Europe?" Callum asked inquisitively.

"I have seen movies and documentaries, we know they are only showing us what they want us to see but most of us know the inner lands are totally controlled and similar to an open prison. Taxes and government do not exist here and if anyone wants to leave or go on vacation, we go to the outer lands."

"Really!" Callum said, giving Leon a raised eyebrows look.

"So how far is it from here to the outer lands then?"

"By air 2 or 3 hours or by ship a couple of days, may I ask where you come from?"

"We are from England, so what about accommodation, is it residential properties only?"

"No Sir, we have certain sections of the island dedicated to housing for the service workers, although many live in at the residences.

Then there are hotels for visitors and crew from the ships. Most the residences are around the edge of the island with some inland but high up in the mountains."

"So what kind of house or apartment do you live in?" Leon asked.

"I have a nice little house and garden with my wife and two children, I don't have to work because everything is provided, including health care and we have a very good hospital, however, I do like to meet new people as it can get a little boring here at times."

"Only one hospital for the whole island?" Callum asked.

"Yes, because we very rarely get sick, however, some of the elderly residents still need their ongoing blood transfusions of young blood to keep them going."

"What about hookers and trafficking?" Leon asked.

"Yes we know it goes on and they are usually kept in the owners residences or at the castle."

"The castle?" Leon exclaimed.

"Yes, at the top of the island centre is a big castle that was built by the Germans many years ago, it is now used by the residents and their guests for parties and orgies and many young girls and boys live up there."

"So, do they ever come out and walk about or go the beach?" Leon asked.

"Not really, they do get taken to the private residences and I've been asked to deliver and return them occasionally. However, because of the ongoing unrest in the inner lands, many of your so called elites have fled and the hotels are nearly full."

"Talking of hotels, do you know of any with rooms still available, we have 6 people on our yacht and need about 4 rooms?" Callum asked.

"Let me make a few calls, I'll stop at the viewpoint a few miles up ahead. This is called the Del Fuego coast road and circles the entire island, there are also a few smaller islands but they are owned by very high net worth individuals like Mr Gates."

"Yes, we were following his yacht this morning."

"Ahh... I see, may I ask if you are building a property here?"

"Not at the moment, we're still trying to understand how it all works here," Callum said, nudging Leon.

"Well, to be allocated an acre of prime land, one must have a net worth of US$100 million dollars, two acres is 200 million and so on. You can then build whatever you like, so long as it's for residential purposes only. Many properties are very beautiful with many acres of grounds, some overlooking the ocean and some are built high up in the forest."

"So, is there a government controlling all this?"

"Not at all, we have military police and a council of elders that meet once a week, all issues that cannot be resolved between the individuals concerned are decided upon by the elders and their decision is final. It is nothing like your court system and we do not have judges or juries."

"So what about crime and jails for the crazies?" Leon asked.

"Yes we have a jail but it is only used as a holding place until they are sent to Dragon Peaks, it is very rare but anyone accused of anything serious like homicide is sent there."

"And where is that then?" Callum asked.

"I have no idea but I have been told, it's a 5 day trip in a cargo vessel and from what I have heard, it is not a nice place to be sent to, very cold and the only other people on the island are other offenders."

"Sounds like the US then," Callum joked.

The taxi stopped at the viewpoint and they all got out to have a good look around. Several smaller islands with one or two very impressive properties were a mile or so further out.

"That is Mr Gates's island," Lorenzo said, pointing to a beautiful split level property that looked like it was built entirely from green glass.

"And the island beyond with the big yacht is Mr Carlos Slim Helu."

"Nice yacht," Callum said smiling.

"Please relax and you may help yourself to drinks and snacks in the restaurant, I will see if I can find some accommodation for you." Lorenzo said, walking away.

Callum and Leon wandered around and realised that they were the only ones acting like tourists and the locals all seemed very happy and contented. The girl in the restaurant was very helpful and even offered to come and work for Callum as he had jokingly told her that he'd just moved to Galeca and was currently building a house there. The scenery at the viewpoint reminded Leon of Kata Noi in Phuket, Thailand where he'd lived for a few months.

About fifteen minutes later, Lorenzo returned and said he'd found a hotel and asked if they wanted to check in as it was only a few miles further around the coast road. Continuing towards the hotel Leon said he was confused about why the locals wanted to work for the psychopathic elites if money was not necessary.

"Maybe, I was not clear because we locals do not work for them, they bring their own staff and when not in residence, their properties are locked up and vacant. The reason I and many other locals take voluntary positions, like driving a taxi or running a shop or restaurant is because we want to interact with others, however we do not have to!" Lorenzo exclaimed.

"I see, so there must be people here, especially youngsters, that want to travel and see the world like Callum and myself?"

"Yes of course, but visiting the inner lands is definitely not desirable, most people who leave Galeca venture to the outer lands."

"But isn't it really cold the further one goes out past Antarctica to the outer lands?"

"Antarctica is cold but then there are other Suns that circle the numerous outer lands. You have many questions and I think you would enjoy listening to Gallen, she is one of our elders and doing a talk at the islands community center this weekend."

"Really! So where is that then?" Leon asked.

"Just ask any taxi driver to take you but it's at the southern tip of the island in Freelanders bay."

"So, who exactly goes to listen to her then?" Leon asked.

"Mostly the locals as the elites are into their own thing, very materialistic and not interested in spiritual progression."

"So, is she religious then?" Callum asked.

"Not at all, religions were created by the controllers and truth be told, most of the elites are... How shall I say... into the dark side!"

"You mean they are Satanists?"

"Yes, we know they use children's blood for transfusions to keep them young but we locals don't approve or get into their abominable practices and all live long healthy lives."

"So Lorenzo, how old are you, if you don't mind me asking?"

"Take a guess?" He replied smiling in the mirror.

"I don't know... maybe 55 or 60," Leon said.

"I'm 95."

"Whoa... Ninety five! but that's impossible!"

"Wait till you see Gallen, she's 178 but looks younger than me!"

Callum and Leon were stunned at his revelation and realised how totally controlled everyone was in the inner world, with chemtrails polluting the air and soil, fluoride and other chemicals in the water, chemicals in the food and the pharmaceutical industry keeping everyone on some kind of medication or using vaccines. The hotel was quaint and set in the hillside surrounded by lush vegetation and overlooking the ocean. Callum booked 4 rooms and told reception they would return later that evening.

The rest of tour was just like driving around Hawaii or any other big island, except for the fact, that all the properties they saw were huge and had large walls to either keep people out or as Callum suggested, it was most likely to keep their slaves in! Callum was quite knowledgeable about the people trafficking industry and said that he knew of at least two warehouses in China and Korea where hundreds of trafficked slaves, mainly young boys and girls were sold to the highest bidders every month.

On arrival back at the marina, they waved off Lorenzo and took the tender back to the Mermaid. Everyone was excited and crowded around to hear what Callum and Leon had to say then after his explanation, he set up a rota so at least 1 of the crew stayed aboard the yacht. Leon said he would do the first night as he wanted to go hear what Gallen had to say at the weekend.

Everyone else jumped in the tender as Callum took them ashore and then onto the hotel.

CHAPTER 9

DAY 2

By 9.30 AM, Callum was back on the Mermaid with Kona, who's turn it was for watch that day and Leon returned to shore with Callum.

"I'm not sure what to do about Jita, she's been going on and on to Nadi about sending a search party out to find Gert but we can't reveal ourselves as they might throw us in the jail!" Callum said to Leon.

"So who would we ask or report it to?"

"I have no idea, there doesn't seem to be any police stations or immigration like all other islands we visited back home and anyway, it would be an impossible task as there are thousands of miles of nothing out there, but I didn't have the heart to tell her that after rescuing her."

"I understand but she could get us all in trouble!" Leon exclaimed.

"Exactly, so I've told Nadi to keep a close eye on her, so, are you up for a bit more exploration today? Lorenzo said he'd show us a few celebrities homes."

"Why not, I'm just amazed that virtually nobody seems to know about this place and it's excluded from all the maps!"

Lorenzo was waiting at the hotel in an 8 seater Mercedes people carrier, so after calling Nadi, Mauru and Jita down, off they went.

"I have heard there is much unrest and many riots in your countries and that is why so many elites have travelled to Galeca?" Lorenzo asked.

"Yes, it's like the end times because the new world order is pushing their depopulation agenda," Leon replied.

"And how old do people live for in your countries?" Lorenzo asked.

"It used to be 80 to 85 as the norm but since the Convid scam and mass vaccinations, people and even children are dying of all ages," Leon replied.

"Vaccinations!"

"Yes, they renamed the flu, Covid 19 and told everyone they needed to be vaccinated but then millions got sick and now, the excess deaths every month are staggering!"

"But isn't a cold or the flu, just the body detoxifying itself!" Lorenzo exclaimed.

"Of course, but the powers that should not be, control the media and all governments and their 2030 agenda is to reduce the population from 8 Billion people down to 500 Million." Callum explained.

"Oh dear, that sounds terrible, so why are the elites not dying as well?"

"Because they know exactly what is going on and never took the clot shot," Leon piped in.

"Clot shot?" Lorenzo asked.

"Yes, whatever is in the vax causes various issues like the immune system stops working and people die from turbo cancer, heart attacks, strokes and various blood clots but they are not normal blood clots, they are pulling long white calamari type substances out of people arteries and call them Hydra, undertakers say they are alive!"

"Oh my... that sounds awful!"

"My husband has cancer and we were on our way here, I have to find him?" Jita said out of the blue.

"So where is he now?" Lorenzo asked.

"On our way here we found Jita drifting in a small yacht with a broken mast but her husband was dead and we had to leave him behind." Callum replied.

"But we are going to send out a search party," Jita added as Callum quickly changed the subject.

"So who are these other celebrities that live here then?"

"OK... see that property on the hill to the right, that is David Bowie's and the one with a blue roof, his name is Prince."

"But they are both dead aren't they!" Leon exclaimed.

"Not at all, they also give live performances at the amphitheatre with many more musicians that reside here. I think you need to understand that although many of the elites come and go in their yachts, many people that reside here have retired and live here permanently. I believe they are allowed to stay on condition that they do not return to the inner lands."

"Very interesting," Leon said.

"So who else is here that is supposed to be dead?" Callum asked curiously.

"Quite a lot actually, I took Mr Epstein to Mr Gates's property last night after dropping you off."

Nadi was staring out the window in awe at all the stunning properties but poor Jita was becoming more anxious by the day. The tour lasted two hours and instead of returning to the hotel, Callum asked Lorenzo to drop them all at a stunning restaurant overlooking another marina and dock at the south of the island.

CHAPTER 10

DAY 3

The following morning, two British military policemen were at the hotel asking to see our passports. Leon tried to make conversation with them but they said they were under strict orders to detain them. Callum asked why but they were not at all friendly and said to follow them out to their armoured vehicle. They were then taken to a secure compound and made to wait in individual rooms before being questioned. Half an hour later, Marau who was on watch on the Mermaid, was also brought in and questioned. Callum knew they'd been found out and was hoping they would be allowed to stay, but then the officer in charge came into his room.

"As you know, this is a restricted island and you have somehow slipped through the net because of the amount of boats arriving over the last few days. Normally you would have been warned and turned around, however, as you are here illegally, your boat has been impounded and the island the Governor will decide your fate."

"Will we be sent back then?" Callum asked.

"Not my decision but nobody is sent back from here, the governor will be here shortly," he said, walking out and locking the door.

Half an hour later, they were all brought into another room that was like a small courtroom.

"My name is Kiers Harrison and I am the governor of Galeca. I have looked at your case and you leave me no choice but to send you to Dragon Peaks."

"Where the hell is Dragon Peaks and why can't we just go back to Fiji?" Callum asked.

"Because this island is private territory and all the residents are high net worth individuals. Nobody is allowed to go back to the controlled zone, however, I need to ask where this map we found on your boat came from?" He said, opening up the German Moon map.

"It was Jita's husbands, he was in the German military and was attacked by a drone, we found Jita still alive but left his body on the stranded yacht."

"I see, so he knew all about the German occupied territories?"

"No idea, you need to ask his wife Jita," Callum replied.

"But he was trying to come here to Galeca?" the Governor asked.

"I think so but you killed him and tried to sink their yacht!"

"I don't know the circumstances but he would have been given several warnings to turn around."

"So what happens to my yacht then?" Callum asked.

"If you agree NOT to return to the inner world, you may keep your vessel. You will be escorted to Dragon Peaks and any attempt to return here or to the inner world WILL be met with lethal force."

"So, how many continents are there beyond Antarctica?" Leon asked.

"I am not at liberty to say but you have seen the German map," he said, then indicated for everyone to follow him outside where they were put into two cars to be taken back to the landing dock.

"I trust you have enough provisions onboard and are to follow the container ships through the Summer gate, two armed officers will be joining you onboard so just follow their instructions."

Suddenly Jita jumped up and ran towards him screaming,

"But what about my husband, I have to find him," pushing the governor out of the way, she was out of the door and running with two guards in pursuit.

"No problem, I need to question her further, so the rest of you can get going." he said and walked off.

Leading the rest of us outside, he jumped into a chauffeured Mercedes and disappeared as everyone else was taken back to the Mermaid. Once safely back onboard, Callum tried to talk to the two military guards assigned to accompany them but was told, they were not allowed to discuss or interact and to just make sure we get into the shipping lane.

Heading out into open water, they soon saw another large container ship in the distance and was ordered to steer a course to fall in line behind it.

CHAPTER 11

SUMMER GATE

It was clear that Gert's Moon map was of great interest and Callum was becoming quite excited.

"So what's stopping us overpowering those two goons and sailing away?" Leon asked Callum.

"And where would we go? We can't go back and we don't have the Moon map anymore, actually, have you noticed how low the Sun and Moon are on the horizon and they are kind of ant-arcing away from us."

"Yes, how come they aren't rising in the East and setting in the West!" Leon exclaimed.

"Because the compass is not working down here and kind of proves the flat earth model, the Sun and Moon are simply going around the North pole or most likely, the magnetic mountain under Polaris, the North star that never moves, also destroying the tilted 1000 miles per hour spinning globe narrative."

"So, how come we can't see the North star Polaris, all the stars look different down here!"

"That's because of the visual limits of our eyes, we can't see forever due to varying atmospheric conditions and the distance is probably thousands of miles and the stars we see here, also cannot be seen from say Europe or North America."

"Sorry, I don't get it?" Leon replied.

"Imagine we are in a big room with random lights in a 10 feet high ceiling. Now let's expand that room to say 5 miles wide and looking up, we can both see a group of lights that look like a fish. Now, as you walk away, by the time you are a mile away, the ceiling and floor have merged together at eye level and I can hardly see you, and at 3 miles you are totally invisible to my naked eye. I then call you up on the phone and ask if you can still see the fish constellation on the ceiling and you say, no, I see an elephant but no fish."

"Ahh... yes, I understand."

"The stars all rotate in a counter clockwork direction and seem to be fixed within the dome. As for the planets, that used to be called wandering stars, I have no idea as we are not allowed up there, just like the North and South pole, 60 degrees South actually, unless escorted on an expensive tour, to what they claim to be Antarctica but I think they are just being taken to one of the outer islands like Deception Island, still almost a 1000 miles from the tip of Argentina, appropriate name don't you think?"

"Interesting... So, without an accurate map we could be lost at sea for months." Leon replied.

"Maybe, but if we can keep on a straight heading by using the stars, we have to hit land at some point and what's our alternative? End up on some prison island we cannot escape from and be attacked by the residents all trying to escape! I don't think it would be too difficult to find another continent, according to the Buddhist map, there are loads of big continents surrounding our inner world and countless smaller islands."

"But what do we do about the two guards with guns?"

"Leave it to me, I'll have a word with Nadi but I don't want to kill them or anything, so are you in agreement?"

"Can't think of a better plan, so yeah, let's go for it." Leon replied.

"OK, can you go tell the boys to meet me down in my cabin?"

Callum walked off to find Nadi and went up to the bridge to speak to Marau and Kona.

The two guards were quite relaxed and easy going, except they wouldn't answer any questions regarding where we were heading and had machine guns. They weren't walking around with them all the time and at meal times they sat with everyone else around the table. Nadi had become quite friendly with them and they didn't see her as a threat, so when she asked them if they were married? One of them opened up and said he was, so Nadi then asked if she lived with him on Galeca but he said that she didn't and was back in Oregon in the US.

"So how long do you guys have to be out here for then?" Nadi asked.

"Usually it's a six month tour," one of them replied.

"And do your wives know about the outer lands?"

"Definitely not, all personnel are sworn to secrecy or else we could end up on Dragon Peaks.

"Really, so why can't you tell us about Dragon Peaks?"

"Nothing there basically, just a rocky island similar to Easter Island but bloody freezing as it's thousands of miles away from the second Sun and in the middle of nowhere."

"Second Sun! So how do all the people live?"

"No idea, it's run by the criminals that were sent there, not many survive and the rumour is, they have resorted to cannibalism!"

"Probably sick of eating fish and penguins," the other guard joked.

"From what I've heard, they've built cabins and live in caves but as for food and living conditions, it's pretty harsh to say the least," the first guard continued.

"But why can't you tell us more about where we were headed then?"

"Because we are under strict orders and don't want to be sent there ourselves. That's enough of the questions and count yourself lucky they let you keep your boat."

"But how do you get back after escorting us then?"

"I said, no more questions," he replied angrily, pulling his mate up and both walking out the dining area.

"Do you think they are carrying sidearms?" Leon asked Callum.

"It doesn't look like it but they are most likely well trained or special opps and could easily kill us with their bare hands. Nadi, I'm going to go down to the engine room and I need you to ask them if they could give us a hand as there's a problem with the engine fuel lines. Leon, I need you to come with me and help me bolt the door once I get them inside," Callum said seriously.

Nadi went up top to do as she was asked and Leon followed Callum down to the engine room.

"But you can't lock them in there, they might disable the engine and then we'd be really stranded!"

"Don't worry, there's a smaller side room down there and all I need you to do, is hide behind the door, I'll ask them to get me my tool box or whatever and as soon as they go in, you slam the door and lock them in."

"Are you serious! but what if only one of them goes in?"

"Then lock him in and we can both overpower the other one."

Leon was definitely not happy and thought Callum had lost his mind but did as he asked and hid behind the second door.

"Now, just be quiet until they go in and Nadi has already placed a box of tinned food and water in there so we don't have to open it for a week or so."

Callum started messing around on the engine and disconnected one of the fuel lines causing diesel to spray out. Nadi then walked in with the two men who asked what was wrong?

"The bloody fuel line is leaking, can you get me my tool box in there and some rags, I can't let go or it will spray everywhere."

One of them walked in and picked up the large red toolbox as the other one said,

"So where are the rags then?"

"On the top shelf in a box to your right," Callum shouted.

The second guard walked in and Leon slammed the door shut, quickly locking it from the outside. They could hear the two guards shouting and banging on the door but simply walked back up top.

"OK, you go get their machine guns and I'm going up top to see if any ships are following us, Callum said smiling.

Up on the bridge, Callum pulled out his binoculars and scanned the ocean behind him, the container ship in front was a good 4 or 5 miles away. So as soon as they cleared the Summer gate, a huge crack in the ice wall about 500 metres wide, he steered the Mermaid to Port, then picked a star just becoming visible on the horizon and told Kona to keep heading towards it.

CHAPTER 12

THE AIRSHIP

By midnight, the star that Callum pointed out was almost overhead and he'd drawn out a basic map of the stars he could see and told Kona,

"OK, we are basically heading East South East and need to keep this heading, we need to account for the star rotations, so I now need you to head towards that binary star," Callum pointed.

Marau had joined them on the bridge as it was his turn to take over steering the Mermaid. Callum was still wide awake as were Nadi and Leon, all still pondering over the maps. However, the only one that was showing the continents outside Summers gate had two huge continents about 800 miles, to what he assumed, was to the East and a few smaller land masses to the West. But because it was still in the middle of the night with no Moon in sight, visibility was very low.

By sunrise, Callum estimated that the Summer gate was about 50 miles ahead and to call everyone up on deck. As they followed the container ship through the large opening, Callum noticed that there were no ships behind them and slowly reduced the speed down to 8 knots. The huge ice wall on the port side was at least 150 feet in height, the other side was too far away to estimate but looked equally as high. Everyone was in awe at the beautiful white ice wall that towered over them as Callum mentioned to Leon that he was planning on making a run for it as soon as they exited the passage.

"You know, I've been wondering about that Moon map and it all seems to make sense," Leon said.

"Go on..." Callum replied.

"Well, we know that the bottom section is where all our known continents are clearly shown but what if the dome is much wider and encompasses all the land on the Moon map. It looks to me, like the dome terminates just beyond South Australia and extends over all the land on the Moon map!"

"Yes, it does look weird but if there is a second Sun as that guard confirmed, it would either have to go around further out, making the days and nights much longer or maybe there are other Suns, giving life to other ponds with their own continents and domes that are simply too far away for us to see from the inner world. Well, at least the Moon map shows lots of extra land directly ahead, albeit hundreds of miles, but the last thing we need is to end up back in jail or sent to Dragon Peaks. I suggest we take a chance and head more to the East. I know the compass is useless out here but we could plot a course on the star map."

By mid afternoon, they had exited the Summer gate and although the Sun was almost out of visibility, there was still twilight, as if the dome were wrapping the light but then it became pitch black really quickly and they adjusted their heading to follow the stars on the makeshift star map. However, by midnight, a new sunrise was beginning from a second Sun and as it got closer, Callum noticed it was also ant-arcing away from them but in the opposite direction to the original Sun.

"Well, at least that proves it's on its own circuit I suppose," Leon said to Callum.

"Yes and as we are outside of its circular path, if we head in slightly, we should eventually come across some warmer liveable land."

By 3 AM, it looked like the middle of the day and all their watches and clocks were off kilter but by 6 PM, it was completely dark again as the second Sun quickly disappeared over the horizon.

"What the hell, look at that," Callum pointed up.

A transparent, purple Moon was clearly visible and following the same path as the second Sun. Grabbing his binoculars, Callum focused on it and said,

"It has similar craters but nothing like the patterns on our Moon, definitely transparent though but wait, there's something passing in front or behind it, I can't tell exactly but it looks like a giant airship!"

Handing the binoculars to Leon he said,

"Here, what do you think?"

Leon looked up and after adjusting the focus he said,

"If that's an airship it has to be absolutely huge and hold thousands of people, how far away is that do you think?"

"Well, we know our Moon isn't 250,000 miles away, so, if we can see it with our naked eyes, I'd say no more than 80 miles."

"Maybe we could follow it?" Leon suggested.

"I can see where you're coming from, but what if they can travel thousands of miles, I read that the old airships in the 1800's could stay up for weeks or months on end!"

"Yes and if we change our heading, we could end up in the middle of nowhere but I'm also intrigued to know where it came from and where it's heading. Let's ask everyone what they want to do."

Leon called everyone up on deck and they were in awe, all staring up at the purple Moon, clouds and sky. Callum explained what they'd seen and everyone agreed that following the airship was the best course of action. So, opening the throttle, he aimed the Mermaid towards the airship that had now traversed the Moon and was now heading away from them to Starboard. The purple Moon seemed to be moving faster than the white Moon they all knew, that took all night to traverse the sky, in fact, it was moving twice as fast and the new sunrise was soon upon them. The airship was still in sight and icebergs could be seen in the distance, confirming that the new Sun was making concentric circles, approaching from the Port side, ant-arcing around them and setting in the distance up ahead on the Starboard side. A few hours later the Sun had almost disappeared but the airship was turning and heading directly towards them.

"That thing looks bigger than a bloody cruise ship," Leon exclaimed.

"Yes, but why have they changed course!" he replied looking all concerned.

As the giant airship approached, everyone was on deck staring up at the biggest flying structure they'd ever seen. Easily as long as two cruise ships placed end to end with many rows of what looked like cabins with balconies running the whole length of it. Hundreds of people were seen waving as it hovered about 500 feet just off to the Port side.

"That thing is massive, look at all the rows of portholes, there must be over 10 levels inside!" Leon exclaimed all excitedly.

"And look at all those people waving on the observation platform underneath," Nadi replied.

Callum tried contacting them on the radio but couldn't get any response.

"I say we follow it?" Leon suggested.

"Sounds good to me, better than sailing blind and maybe they will lead us to a more welcoming continent," Callum replied.

"This is unbelievable, obviously we've been lied to on a massive scale as almost everyone believes we live on a spinning water ball in the vacuum of space but this proves there are other worlds and continents beyond Antarctica. And have you noticed the Sun out here is a more orange colour and as it approaches from the left, it kind of ant-arcs in front of us and heads off towards our right," Leon said.

"That makes sense, it's doing the same thing as our Sun when we were on the other side of the ice wall. I think the globe psyop is dead and the inner earth is a huge open air farm. Obviously, some people or entities, know the reality of where we live but have created a prison planet called Earth but what if the earth IS the basement of the universe and there are infinite worlds or continents to explore?" Callum replied.

"Sounds much more feasible than stars like our Sun with rotating planets that are so far away that it would take 32,000 years travelling at 100,000 miles per hour just to get a 25th of the way to the nearest star!"

"Exactly! But convince everyone they live on a planet in outer space and there is no more land, then you have a totally controlled population. That's why they put the Antarctic treaty in place, so nobody can independently explore below 60 degrees South."

"Look, it's turning," Leon said, pointing up.

"OK, well if it's operating like a cruise ship, they must be on some kind of tour of the inner lands and if we follow it from a distance, they could lead us to a more friendly group of people."

"But what if there are lands like Earth where everyone is fighting and trying to take over other countries and resources!" Leon exclaimed.

"I'm sure not everywhere is going to be easy and harmonious, even the best places in our inner world like the USA or Australia have their fair share of conflict and slum areas. My research has shown that all the wars and conflicts in our world are all manufactured to thin out the population and create division between the people. Imagine millions or even billions of people, waking up and coming together and saying NO to the controllers. The only reason they are able to control everyone is because of the lies and propaganda they program everyone with from birth, like we live on a ball in the vacuum of space and that democracy is real, when the real truth is, all presidents and people in positions of power are selected not elected. I think the people or entities that control us, know exactly how this fake world we find ourselves in actually works. They also have incredible technology like Directed Energy Weapons and things we can't even imagine and have no intention of sharing them with us the masses. They know all about karma and reincarnation and created all the religions to simply distract and divide the people. They also want to keep this amazing world for themselves and every 140 years have to do a reset to depopulate."

"Like the Spanish flu in the 1800's or was it the 1900's?" Leon asked.

"It wasn't the flu, it was the vaccinations, just like the con-vid bullshit. The problem is, 95% of the population believe the government is there to look after them but in reality, they are there to control and keep everyone working, in debt and paying endless taxes."

"Definitely and I always wondered why there were different races like Asian, Caucasian and Negro but now it all makes perfect sense. I bet there are continents full of Asians or Negro type races."

"That reminds me of a video I saw recently, it was explaining how the Sun migrated outwards and every few thousand years, a new Sun is born from the North Pole, I think it was titled, The Outward flow of Civilizations with David Weiss and Sofia Smallstorm."

Everyone was now on deck and watching the huge airship heading away as Callum told Kona to follow but keep a good couple of miles behind. By nightfall, the Sun had disappeared into the distance and the beautiful purple Moon was lighting up the sky and clouds. The markings were also different to the Moon they knew from the inner world and confused Callum and Leon even more.

"Look at that!" Kona said all excitedly, pointing towards a huge craft passing in front of the Moon.

"Wow! That must be far bigger than the airship we're following," Leon replied.

Looking through his binoculars, Callum then said,

"Looks bigger than three aircraft carriers placed end to end and I can see lots of smaller craft buzzing around as well," handing the binoculars to Leon.

"I hope they're friendly," Nadi said, hugging Callum.

As the sky became dark, all the stars positions were also different to the inner world, no big dipper or known constellations could be recognised. This fact alone made Callum think that the dome must be far lower and wider than they originally thought, more like a large dinner plate than a dome that only covered the inner lands and terminated just beyond Antarctica.

By midnight everyone had gone below, leaving Leon up top keeping watch and following the airship. Marvelling at the cloudless black sky with millions of tiny stars, some of them twinkling with bright flashes of colour.

CHAPTER 13

FAERFENG BAY, VUCRUANIA

Callum took over the wheel at 5 AM, allowing Leon to go down to get some sleep. The bright orange Sun was approaching from the left again and by 6.10 it was completely daylight and moving slowly towards them. The airship was slowing down as more land could just be seen up ahead. Pulling out his binoculars, he saw that the land had tropical foliage and huge palm trees with houses or buildings built into the hillside. Nadi had now joined him on deck with Kona and Marau, all taking turns with the binoculars until Maru said that he could see boats.

"Take the wheel," Callum said, taking the binoculars and having a good look.

"Looks like a town or village but their boats are very similar to ours and coming out of what looks like a port or marina of some kind but the airship looks like it's docking onto a tall tower."

As they pulled down the main sails, they continued sailing until they saw the opening to a semi circular coastal lagoon. Hundreds of small boats were moored up along 8 lines of jetties and about 12 larger boats were anchored in the lagoon. About half an hour later they entered the lagoon and saw a small town with people now disembarking from the airship, going inside the tall structure then exiting at the bottom.

"I think they are having a stopover and letting some passengers off to have a walk about. Strangely there are no police or immigration but they look friendly enough, I'm gonna get a bit closer then drop anchor," Callum said to Leon.

The airship was moored to a tower by it's nose, facing into the wind and what looked like, hundreds of people disembarking. The scenery was amazing and looked very similar to Vietnam with limestone islands everywhere but not as hot. Callum dropped anchor and told Kona and Marau to stay aboard while Nadi, Callum and Leon ventured ashore.

Luckily they blended in and most of the people seemed to be Caucasian and blond. However, there were other races but the thing they noticed most, was that some of the people were extremely tall. Most of the people milling around were the same as them but the tall ones seemed to be dressed differently and dark haired. Easily over ten feet in height and walking around as if everything was completely normal.

Callum tied their tender to the dock and they all stepped ashore then walked down the jetty towards the small town. Buses were ferrying the airship passengers down from the tower on the hill and the town reminded Callum of Positano, a stunning white hillside village community in Southern Italy. Hundreds of houses and shops were built into the hillside with little lanes and thousands of steps. However, all the shops and many of the houses had huge doorways, probably to accommodate the taller residents.

"Did you hear their language? I think it's German!" Callum exclaimed.

Leon agreed but as neither of them could speak or understand German, they had no idea what was being said. Nadi wanted to check out a boutique and went inside as Leon and Callum began looking at some strange vegetables on a market stall. They also saw money changing hands but it seemed to be different coloured coins. On closer inspection, he saw they were most likely gold, silver and copper or bronze with intricate patterns. Nadi came out of the boutique and waved Callum and Leon over, following her inside, an old lady greeted them in a strange accent but she spoke English.

"Welcome to Faerfeng Bay, my name is Gavay and your lovely lady here tells me you come from the inner world?"

"Yes, nice to meet you and what county is Faergeng Bay part of?" Callum asked.

"We don't have countries like your world but Faereng Bay is part of Vucruania, a continent the size of Australia in your world. May I offer you some refreshments? I haven't met anyone from the inner world for ages, so where exactly are you from?" Gavay asked.

"Well, Leon and I are from England and Nadi is from Fiji," Callum replied.

"And how did you escape? If you don't mind me asking."

"Long story but we need to know where we are and if it's safe to stay in Vucruania."

"Oh yes, you're safe here but there are other lands that are more restrictive yet nothing like your world."

"But how come you know about our world?" Nadi asked.

"Because I was married to a man that came here from America but he died about 30 years ago, he also escaped and we lived together until he died at age 87."

"Sorry but you don't look old enough to have been married and..." Callum said, stopping mid sentence.

"Yes I understand, I'm 168 and met my husband when I was 104," Gavay replied smiling.

"But you only look about 50!" Nadi exclaimed.

"Thank you my dear, but here in the outer lands we live much longer as we are not being sprayed and poisoned by your controllers. My husband died from cancer, he said it was the vaccinations he was made to take while serving in the navy. Actually, I don't know of anyone from the inner world that lived longer than 90."

"So, you've met other people like us then?" Leon asked.

"Oh yes, but not for about 50 years or so, something to do with the Antarctica treaty which was introduced around that time, prior to that, we had many explorers."

"What about money and banks?" Leon asked.

"Yes we use money but we don't have banks, everyone is allocated some land at birth and can build a home or whatever but we do not buy or sell land and corporations do not exist here. Money is used as a medium of exchange but barter is the main method."

"So, I can't come along and buy a nice big house overlooking the ocean then?"

"No, but you can exchange your land with someone else and build the house of your dreams. People also exchange houses if they want to go and live in another part of Vucruania."

"And where is the next major continent from here?" Callum asked.

"There are so many continents and even I don't know what lies beyond Vucruania but my husband told me, he believed there are thousands and maybe infinite! However, some of them are not so friendly and we often hear about invasions and land grabs by the Nephalimia but some continents are extremely dark due to not having a close Sun and the people live underground in huge cities and from what I've heard, their Sun moved outwards creating new areas where people can live and grow food like here. Then there is a place called Trau Skya that has a red Sun and 3 green Moons, they are probably the most evil and have been reported to invade other lands, kill all the men and capture all the women and children."

"So, is that within a few days or weeks travel from here?" Callum asked.

"Not at all, they are a long way from Vucruania, maybe 6 months sailing but they also have airships, air planes and large military type warships. Most of the outer worlds have advanced technology and live in peace but there are a few, like Trau Skya and Nephalimia that are always causing problems as they have very advanced weapons and technology."

"That sounds like the Nephilim, a giant race that supposedly controls our world from secret underground bases in Antarctica according to many researchers," Callum replied.

"My husband believed that to be true also, the Nephalimia are at least three times bigger and taller than us."

"Have you ever heard about Dragon Peaks, it's supposed to be a prison island that we were being escorted to?" Leon asked.

"I'm afraid I don't know anything about that but my husband had a map," she said, walking over to a cabinet and pulling out a large wooden box.

Opening the map revealed over a thousand continents and smaller islands surrounding our known inner world and as they began looking for Dragon Peaks, a loud explosion was heard and some kind of siren was turned on.

"What's going on?" Callum asked.

"I don't know but it means we must all go to the bunker," Gavay replied, looking worried.

"Bunker! Why?"

"Follow me, it's inside the mountain and we'll be safe there."

Following her down a long winding pathway, Callum told Leon

and Nadi to be ready to make a run for the boat.

"Does this happen often?" Leon asked Gavay.

"Not for many years because we have a strong deterrent but I heard that the Skya have similar weapons and have been known to attack other lands."

"What kind of weapons?" Callum asked.

"They have laser energy weapons and can destroy huge areas but we have similar technology and the last time they tried to attack us, they were obliterated."

"LOOK AT THAT!" Leon shouted, pointing up at what looked like an alien mother ship from a fantasy movie but even bigger than the airship.

"How the hell does that thing stay up in the air? It's absolutely massive and must be using some kind of anti gravidic technology," Callum replied.

People were re-boarding the airship but the huge mother ship then fired a bright red beam and the airship it burst into flames.

"Quickly, we have to get in the bunker!" Gavay said panicking.

The alien craft was just hovering over the ocean about 10 miles out and as the siren stopped, an eerie silence ensued. Callum realized that they needed to get away ASAP and shouted for everyone to get back to the boat. Running as fast as they could, they managed to get aboard, pull up the anchors and motor away. More explosions were heard and Leon was looking through the binoculars at the massive floating mother ship firing red laser beams.

"That thing could blow the whole town to smithereens!" Leon exclaimed.

"Exactly, that's why we're getting out of here," Callum replied.

"Now there are small triangular craft coming out of it," Leon continued.

As they all watched, the smaller craft headed to the island and began firing lasers at the buildings and then a new, much faster siren was heard. Watching in awe, a huge circular opening appeared at the top of the mountain and it was like something out of Star Wars as white beams of light emanated out and the small craft began falling out of the skies. Then a huge green laser beam was fired at the mother ship but it hit some kind of impenetrable force field. The mother ship then fired a similar beam back which blew half of the mountain away. Thousands of small and large rocks were raining down on the boat as everyone ran inside for cover. Then as they all stared at the ongoing laser battle, another laser was fired from a different part of the mountain. This time it hit the mother ship as their force field must have been turned off temporarily as it was still firing. The massive ship was now on fire and banked to the left before heading away at speed.

"That was insane, but what on earth possesses them to attack other countries when those countries also have similar weapons!" Leon exclaimed.

"No idea! But it just goes to show that it's not only our inner world that has other entities trying to take over their land or control them."

Suddenly they heard what sounded like jet fighters but they were small and triangular in shape and going after the warship. Laser beams were fired and after a few minutes, the warship banked to the left and dived down into the ocean.

Everyone was in awe as the massive mother ship hit the water but it was too far away to see if it was sinking and looked like it simply entered the water and disappeared.

EPILOGUE

Callum had taken the new map that Gavay had shown them during the panic to get to the bunker and as they sailed off into open water, he pulled it out as everyone crowded around to take another look.

The inner world was approximately 100,000 miles in diameter but only covered a tiny fraction in the center of the new map, with thousands, if not, tens of thousands of islands and continents spreading outwards. Callum estimated that the map they were looking at was at least 2 million miles in diameter and probably continued outwards off the map even further.

Although many of the continents had recognisable planet names like Venus, Jupiter and Neptune but Callum then found Nephalimia, which was on the opposite side of the map to where they were in Vucruania. Leon then found Trau Skya which was also a long way from Vucruania but near the outer edge of the map.

Callum then plotted a course towards Islas Libras, the next major continent about 1500 miles further out and their real adventure had only just begun.

###

ABOUT THE AUTHOR

Dave James was born in the UK and is an adventurer and entrepreneur who currently lives in Thailand. He has authored several books on the True Earth, Freedom, The Game of Life, Thailand related scams and horror stories and has been an Astrological consultant for over 40 years.

James's travels include living and working in the USA, Italy, France, Germany, Holland, Spain, South Africa, India, The Philippines, Indonesia, Australia, New Zealand and Thailand.

OTHER BOOKS BY THIS AUTHOR

Please visit your favourite e-book retailer to discover other books by Dave James

Escape from Tyranny : True Earth and the search for more land beyond the Antarctic ice ring.
Treasure Hunters - Spanish Gold of the San Martinez
Treasure Hunters - Tika's Revenge (Follow up book)
Astrology of Transgender's Relationships and Compatibility: Synastry, Transits and Reincarnation
Everyone is Asleep : But a few have woken up and live lives of total amazement
Lambs to the Slaughter : Love, Scams and True stories of Thai girls
Lambs to the Slaughter : 2
Lambs to the Slaughter : 3
Freedom in Thailand : How we escaped and built a bungalow and pool resort
Attracting Your Soulmate or Special Partner : By Asking the Universe and or Astrology
Life Is An IQ Test : And virtually everything you think you know is a lie because of propaganda and mass mind control
The Fall of the Great Reset: Rise of the Pure Bloods
What Is This Realm?: And what happens when we die? Are we in a soul trap or simulation?
The Apartment: A voyeur on the run from the Triads in Hong Kong
The Globe Lie: And Understanding the Matrix of Illusion

The Assassin's Daughter: An eye for an eye

CONNECT WITH DAVE JAMES

I really appreciate you reading my book!

Amazon Author page : https://www.amazon.co.uk/Dave-James/e/B08BL3SDSR

www.DaveJames.uk

Email me at: davespersonalmail@gmx.com

www.ingramcontent.com/pod-product-compliance
Ingram Content Group UK Ltd.
Pitfield, Milton Keynes, MK11 3LW, UK
UKHW022012190726
13853UKWH00004B/1898